GW01402625

Living
with
flowers

Living with flowers

PAMELA HAMILTON

ANGUS
& ROBERTSON
PUBLISHERS

ANGUS & ROBERTSON PUBLISHERS

Unit 4, Eden Park, 31 Waterloo Road,
North Ryde, NSW, Australia 2113, and
16 Golden Square, London W1R 4BN,
United Kingdom

First published in Australia
by Angus & Robertson Publishers in 1988

Published by arrangement with
Bacragas Pty Ltd

Copyright © Pamela Hamilton 1988
  ISBN 0 207 15853 3.

Designed by Lynda Christie
and Sue Maybury.
Typeset in 11pt Galliard by
The Type Shop Pty. Limited
Printed in Australia
at Griffin Press Limited

CONTENTS

INTRODUCTION

A love of flowers, a flair for design and pottery, and a passion for antiques resulted in my lifetime involvement with floral art and the collecting of flower containers. The enjoyment of arranging flowers for my own home or for special events expanded into exhibiting, lecturing and visiting flower shows all around the world.

While I admire formal arrangements I believe that simple ones can be just as lovely. Both my mother and grandmother loved flowers and I remember with pleasure the wonderful prodigality with which they made "traditional" arrangements with flowers and foliage gathered from their own gardens. Today the trend towards smaller gardens, inner-city living and busy work schedules has meant less time and fewer opportunities to grow one's own flowers; there have also been changes in the type of furniture we use and the general decor we choose for our homes. Flowers are expensive to buy so today we use them more sparingly; the "mood" of an arrangement often has to be in accord with streamlined furniture — marble, leather, glass and chrome.

The art of flower-arranging lies in the creation of a "picture" which suits its surroundings and makes full use of the individual beauty of the flowers used.

There is nothing like the joy of seeing a room take on grace when an arrangement is just right. Flowers add to the quality of life and the floral artist is fortunate in having such lovely material with which to be creative.

CHAPTER ONE

THE BASIC PRINCIPLES OF FLORAL ART

Flower-arranging should be something more than just putting pretty flowers into a vase; a perfectly composed arrangement can be a minor work of art. All fine art is governed by certain principles, and anyone who loves flowers and enjoys presenting them will find it well worth while taking a little time and trouble to acquaint themselves with these basic rules, for, once understood and appreciated, applying them will become second nature. Design, proportion, balance, harmony, repetition, rhythm, accent and unity all play their part in the creation of a perfect work of art. The floral artist has another consideration — texture.

DESIGN

The design of an arrangement is its line. Line is based on the simple laws of

Above: A modern arrangement of scarlet anthuriums, clipped fan-palm leaves and rounded calathea leaves, set against an unusual background of pieces of mirror glass and red and white perspex. The square black lamp base lights up the arrangement.

Australian native banksia, gumnuts and small leafed blue-grey eucalyptus foliage blend well with driftwood and a slate base. The swirls of driftwood can be enjoyed for their own sculptured beauty.

geometry which govern the creation of abstract shapes, both curved and angular. The shape or line of an arrangement can be vertical, horizontal, triangular, diagonal, circular, oval, fan-shaped, crescent-shaped and curved. The line of an arrangement must always be clean and uncluttered, leading the eye effortlessly from one point of interest to another.

PROPORTION

Each component of an arrangement must relate in size to all the others, and the whole arrangement must relate in size to the background against which it is set. Bad proportion looks "wrong". For instance, a tall vase with some short-stemmed flowers just protruding from its neck makes the eye uneasy, and if the vase is jammed into a narrow niche with no headroom, it will look even worse. Although there is no hard and fast rule, flowers and foliage should be about two and a half times the height of their container; if the container is heavy and the arrangement light and airy, the latter can be even taller.

A simple demonstration of what things being "in proportion" means is to take three flowering stems in the hand and to hold them with the flowers one above the other. The second one is held at only two-thirds the height of the first one, and the third at only two-thirds the height of the second one. Holding the stems firmly together, cut them all through at the same place. You will now have stems of three different lengths and no matter where you place them in an arrangement, either vertically, horizontally or triangularly, they will always look "right" in relationship to each other.

BALANCE

Balance, a matter of visual impression, is achieved when size, colour, texture and line combine to create an impression of stability and repose.

Symmetrical balance is an equal balance of weight on either side of an imaginary perpendicular line drawn through the centre of an arrangement. It is generally used in the formal settings made for church decoration, receptions and weddings. The focus of the design is low and in the centre and brought slightly forward to give depth to the arrangement.

Assymmetrical balance is more subtle and less solidly formal. The material on either side of the imaginary axis is dissimilar but the visual effect of equal weight is conveyed by the counterbalance of "heavy" and "light" flowers and strong and pastel colours. Double flowers are "heavier" than single ones; dark colours are "heavier" than pale ones. For example, a dark-red fully blown rose on one side of an arrangement would need several flowers of a daintier type and paler colour on the other side if the desired stability and repose is to be created.

Self-contained balance is achieved when a design, either symmetrical or as-symmetrical depends on structure alone for balance.

Balance by placement requires the greatest amount of plant material and the general flow of linear interest to be on the same side as the greatest area of the base on which the arrangement is set.

HARMONY

Flowers, foliage, container and setting must always look at peace with each other — there must be no jarring note.

REPETITION

The repeated use of a certain shape, colour or line can be very effective if skilfully used. To avoid monotony you can modify a colour by using lighter and darker shades of it; to modify shape use a number of small, round flowers as a repeat of one large one. The important thing is to avoid a "regimented" look. Repetition is used for emphasis, but the emphasis should be subtle.

RHYTHM

The "rhythm" of an arrangement is the way it takes the eye effortlessly around it so that the picture "flows" into the mind without any distraction. A gradual change in size, colour, texture or form of flowers grouped together and the choice of a definite "line" play a large part in attaining the best results. A horizontal design is restful, an upright one dignified and dramatic, and a curving line has gaiety and grace. In all cases the eye should be "led", never "pulled" by sudden contrasts of shape or colour. If you put a flower of one colour between two of another colour, rhythm is lost; it is also lost if short, coarse leaves are placed next to delicate lacy ones.

ACCENT

All designs need a focal point from which creation springs; the arrangement needs a heart and core, a dominant note. You cannot have different colours and different shapes fighting each other for attention if the composition of the arrangement is to have structure and beauty. Nor can any part of the arrangement be allowed to dominate to the detriment of the flow of the main design — the total concept must always be held in the mind.

UNITY

Unity has much in common with harmony; every part of an arrangement must be in accord; container, material, setting must merge so that there is no awareness of their "separateness". For instance, if you have exotic flowers, do not use an eye-catching container and then place the whole thing against a background of highly patterned wallpaper. Unity can be easily lost if the vase which holds the flowers is as interesting as the flowers themselves. There has to be a

For a flower arrangement to be pleasing to the eye, the flowers must be arranged in proportion. If the stems of the flowers are cut to the right length successful arranging is easier.

Above left: Hold three flowers, one above the other, each two-thirds the height of the other. Holding stems firmly together cut all of them in the same place.

Above centre: Flowers arranged in proportion vertically.

Above right: The same flowers arranged proportionally in a triangle.

Two tall pieces of castor-oil plant with stalks stripped of leaves create a modern look when combined with begonia flowers and foliage.

Australian native flower arrangements are tougher than most because they last well and dry well. They link and blend compatibly with driftwood, cork and elm and complement modern designs.

balance of interest, but not equal interest. The unity of an arrangement depends on the correct application of the basic principles.

TEXTURE

Surface finish can be rough or smooth, dull or glossy, velvety, hairy, coarse or fine. A flower arrangement should have textural harmony but not monotony, and thought should be given to any accessories used to complement it as well as to the texture of the walls and curtains which form the setting.

COLOUR

The most perfectly executed floral arrangement will be a failure if the colours of the flowers do not balance. Just as scale and proportion are vital to the perfect design, so is the correct relationship between the shades, tones, tints, and hues of the flowers.

THE LANGUAGE OF COLOUR

Hue, the property by which one colour family is distinguished from another, is usually called "colour". Pure colour that is found in the spectrum does not include black or white.

Tints are colours that contain pure colour (or hue) and white.

Shades are colours that contain pure colour (or hue) and black.

Tones are colours that contain pure colour (or hue) and grey.

Value is the quality of lightness or darkness found in colour. Tints have light (high) value, shades have dark (low) value, and colour at full strength has middle value. Between white and black are the achromatic greys. Between light and dark values are the middle values of each hue.

Chroma is the degree of strength or weakness of a hue.

Full chroma is the hue of greatest strength.

Black, white and grey are considered neutral "colours".

Colour can not only affect our emotions, but also can alter our response to the environment. A hot and stuffy room can seem much cooler if the eye can rest on an arrangement of pale flowers and leaves, delicately arranged in a large bowl of clear water which contains a piece of water-soaked rock and some sparkling pieces of ice-like crystal. In contrast, a cold day will seem much warmer if the room is brightened by the cheerfulness of red, orange and yellow flowers. Large flowers in strong, bold colour give vitality to their surroundings; delicate flowers in pastel shades create a feeling of peace.

THE COLOUR WHEEL

If you study a colour wheel you will find colour and its effects easier to understand. Colour is the general term. The wheel is divided into 12 segments:

1. Primary colours — red, yellow, blue.
2. Secondary colours — orange, green, violet.
3. Intermediate colours — red-orange, yellow-orange, yellow-green, blue-green, blue-violet, red-violet.

The primary colours (hues) are pure ones, with no addition of black or white. Any two primary colours mixed together will form a secondary colour; for example, red mixed with yellow makes orange; yellow mixed with blue makes green; red mixed with blue makes violet. Red, yellow, blue, orange, green and violet are known as "standard hues."

Intermediate colours are made by mixing primary and secondary colours together and they take the name of both of them, for example, red-orange, yellow-green, etc.

Red, orange and yellow are known as "advancing colours" — the warm ones. Green blue and violet are known as the "receding colours" — the cool ones.

Chromatic colours have hue and chroma. Achromatic colours do not — they are the neutral ones, black, white and grey.

Adjacent hues are those lying next to each other on the colour wheel.

Analagous hues are those lying near to each other on the colour wheel — "neighbours".

Colours considered "directly complementary" are those lying opposite each other on the colour wheel. These make the most impact when used in modern floral art; for example, purple and yellow, red and green, blue and orange.

The more proficient you become in the mechanics of making a flower arrangement, the more a "feeling" for colour will grow. A vague discontent about the effect you have produced will crystallise and you will know *what* is wrong.

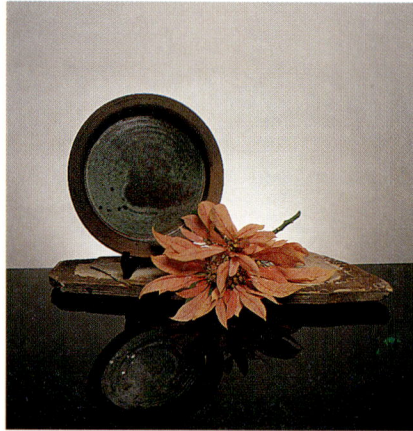

CHAPTER TWO

EQUIPMENT AND MECHANICS

I t is advisable to obtain tools at the outset. Many of the things you need you will have on hand anyway, others will have to be bought. A rough guide to the things you are likely to need is as follows:

1   Japanese butterfly scissors (hasami) to cut flower stems without crushing them.

2   Small pruning saw for larger branches. A mangled cut on a branch can look unsightly.

3   Florist's wire, 16 and 18 gauge, for insertion in hollow stems and general support.

4   Orchid tubes. These are invaluable for positioning short-stemmed flowers high up in an arrangement.

5   Small hammer for splitting stems.

6   Toothpicks for tiny supports.

7   Mister or spray to help to keep flowers fresh and give them that appealing "dewy" look.

8   Florist's tape in green and brown for giving invisible support.

9   Needle-holders in many different shapes and sizes.

10 Pliers and tin-snips, stapler, pins, pipe cleaners, plastic sheets, sticky tape, bath towels, knives — all the common-sense implements that will make small jobs easy and eliminate mess.

11 Plastic buckets for flowers and foliage to stand in while awaiting arrangements.

12 Deep sink in which foliage can be

Above: A handmade pottery plate and a slate base form an elegant arrangement with a salmon-pink bloom of poinsettia.

completely immersed.

13 Oasis. This is an absolute must if flowers are to be given the support they need in a particular arrangement.

14 Skewers and pencils for making the holes in the oasis into which the flower stems are to be inserted.

15 Floral glue for securing the petals of dried flowers into place.

16 Floral clay for holding pin-holders in position.

17 Twist ties for holding flowers, cup-holders, etc, into position.

18 An assortment of pebbles and stones to hide pin-holders.

19 Lengths of fine bamboo, cut into requisite lengths, to give flowers support.

20 A can each of black, gold and silver paint. This is useful for disguising cup-holders, etc.

21 Small watering-can with long curving spout for topping up the water in arrangements.

22 Cup-holders.

23 Candle cup-holders.

24 Sand. You will often find that an arrangement needs stability. Sand is also needed if you are making a floral ''saucer''.

25 Rose-thorn strippers. While these are not essential, there will be times when you wish you had them.

As you proceed you will find small items of equipment that suit you.

NEEDLEHOLDERS

These are the Japanese *kensans* and are considered by most floral artists to be indispensable. The holders have a very heavy lead base which is closely set with sharply pointed steel nails. Flowers can be inserted on and between the nails and will be held in position. You can buy them in different shapes and sizes; circles, crescents, squares, etc, which range from small to large. Some are designed to interlock, which greatly increases their usefulness.

Since the mechanics of how the flowers are held in position have to be hidden it is important to choose the correct size of needle-holder for an arrangement; nothing spoils the appearance of a lovely arrangement than the intrusion of spiked metal. Painting needle-holders black or the colour of the container in which the arrangement is displayed is one way of decreasing their visibility. They can also be covered with black tissue paper or hidden by small pebbles or the discreet placement of short-stemmed leaves angled to look part of the design. Do not use a lot of bits and pieces to conceal a holder. A single piece of a strap-like leaf, such as that of the gladiolus, can be wrapped around the circumference of the holder and will form a green well deep enough to hide the flower stalks.

Needle-holders should always be fixed into position when they and the container are perfectly dry. Floral clay gives far better results than plasticine, which should only be used in emergencies. One method is to press three small balls of clay strategically onto the flat lead base of the needle-holder, then position the holder in the container and press firmly into place.

Protect your fingers from the sharp needles by using a second holder, base upwards, to press down on. Alternatively, roll a long, snake-like piece of clay around the circumference of the needle-holder with enough at the bottom to enable it to adhere to the container, and press firmly into position. In this case it is particularly important that everything should be dry. Check to see whether the join is firm by holding the container upside down; if the whole thing is going to fall apart it is better it should do so now than when water has been added and your arrangement is in position.

Needle-holders will give stability when an arrangement is top-heavy. Two holders, points pressed together, make a heavy lead weight which can be placed in the bottom of a container.

Needle-holders are very useful if you wish to use candles as part of your floral arrangement for an evening meal. You can buy a fitting which can be fixed into a needle-holder and used to hold a candle. Or you can just heat a needle-holder so that the needles are hot enough to penetrate the wax base of the candle easily. You can also use plastic hair-rollers or a small tube of chicken wire — they will hold a candle reasonably steady if you are careful.

You can also use a needle-holder to give weight to the base of a tall vase and then arrange the flowers in a piece of water-soaked oasis which has been cut to fit the neck of the vase. It is wise to cover the oasis with chicken wire or aluminium foil to prevent it disintegrating. Needless to say, these mechanics should be out of sight no matter which angle the vase is viewed from. If you want to use a particular vase but find it is too tall for the flower stems, partly fill the vase with sand and position a needle-holder in it at the height you think is needed, add water and arrange the flowers in the holder. Or you can make a sling of chicken wire deep enough to go about one-third of the way down the container and fix it with florist's wire or ties, and place the holder at the bottom of the sling. The leaves of the arrangement will hide the wire. Plastic-covered wire will be kinder to your vases and your hands.

It is important to buy holders in which the needles are set close together and to keep the needles clean and straight. There is a special Japanese tool for straightening the needles and this is more effective than trying to use a skewer to do the job.

CUP-HOLDERS

These small, round metal containers, painted or unpainted, are also available in brass or chrome. They are about 4 cm deep and have a needle-holder soldered to the base. You can, if you wish, make your own by jamming a needle-holder into the top of an aerosol can of the same circumference. They are very useful for arrangements in china comports, baskets, etc. They can be used, suitably concealed, and fastened to a support, to present short-stemmed flowers high in an arrangement, or they can be concealed behind driftwood or a piece of rock on a base. They hold little water so they will have to be kept topped up if the flowers are to remain fresh.

CANDLE-HOLDERS

These small containers are shaped to fit into a candlestick, the top of a bottle or the narrow neck of a vase. It is wise to secure them into position with floral clay. You can paint them and the clay so that they are inconspicuous.

They can hold a needle-holder or a piece of oasis into which flowers can be inserted. If you are using oasis, cover it with chicken-wire mesh and wire it to the container; also be certain that the weight of the flowers will not cause the container to topple over.

Some have a threaded fitting which enables them to be screwed into a lamp base to convert it into a floral container.

OASIS

Oasis or ''florist's foam'' is used by commercial florists for most of their arrangements. The spongy substance holds several times its own weight of water, will keep flowers fresh for days, and enables them to be positioned safely. It is available in large blocks and smaller shapes. If you have to cut oasis, always do so when it is dry and use a sharp knife. Leave it to soak for several hours before you use it so that it can absorb the maximum amount of water. Soaked oasis can be kept in a plastic bag in the refrigerator for later use.

Since it is continually having holes made in it to accommodate flower stems, it doesn't last too long, but most people find it well worth the expense. To prevent it disintegrating prematurely, wrap it in small-mesh chicken wire. You can make neat holes to receive the flower stalks by using a small skewer or thin pencil — this will also ensure that the stalks can slip in easily without damage. All thick stems should be shaved to a neat point.

Oasis can convert almost anything into a flower container and is particularly suited for use with shells and delicate porcelain, which would be damaged with a heavy needle-holder or a scratchy piece of chicken wire. It is ideal for use with marble or onyx containers, and comports that do not hold water. It is less expensive in the long run than buying needle-holders, and if you have to make a number of arrangements for a wedding or a charity function, using oasis will save you the chore of having to pick up all your vases and equipment the next day.

WIRE NETTING

Chicken-wire gauge is 2.5 cm; turkey-wire gauge is 5 cm. Both have their uses. The smaller gauge is used for thin-stemmed arrangements and for keeping oasis together. The larger one is for use in large urns and vases. It can be used in conjunction with needle-holders or by itself. Used alone it should be rolled tightly, packed firmly into the container and secured into place with florist's wire. You would naturally not use the netting in any container you did not wish to suffer scratching, plastic-covered wire would serve the purpose better and, even then, it would be advisable to line your precious vessels with greaseproof paper or softly crumpled cooking foil.

CHAPTER THREE

CONDITIONING, PRESERVING AND DYEING FLOWERS AND FOLIAGE

There is little that is more aggravating than to find that an arrangement on which much time and thought has been spent, is beginning to droop within a few days. It is wise not only to use fresh flowers and foliage but to take steps to make sure they stay in condition for as long as possible. If you gather flowers from your own garden, pick them early in the morning or when the sun has gone down and the sap in the plants has receded. Take a bucket of water into the garden with you so that no time is lost in giving them their

Above: An arrangement for a hall table. The bright colours of pink may flowers, yellow chrysanthemums and bromeliads with elk-horn foliage give a feeling of warmth and welcome.
Right: A plastic bowl containing water-soaked oasis is fixed to the top of the spaghetti jar. Scarlet waratah, white flannel flowers, blackboy, aralia leaves and dried elkhorn fern — all Australian natives — stand tall on a coffee table.

first drink. Some scissors pinch the stems and damage the cells and ducts, so use a really sharp knife, flower secateurs or the Japanese flower scissors, *hasami*, which are specially designed for this purpose.

Cut all stems on the slant and strip away all the leaves on the lower part of the stems; they would become slimy under water and encourage the growth of bacteria. Since plants lose so much water through their leaves, only keep the leaves you feel are essential for the look of the arrangement you propose to make. As soon as all the flowers are picked, take the bucket to a cool place away from both draughts and sunlight.

Separate the flowering stems from ones with just foliage. Most foliage can be left completely submerged in water. However, soft leaves that are likely to become soggy should be kept dry but with as much of the stem as possible in water.

Flower stems can be soft and fleshy, woody, hollow or milky; the required treatment differs in each case. The methods used are detailed below, followed by a list of the most commonly used flowers and a key to the way the stems should be treated.

Method 1: Water-cutting. This is the cutting of a stem while it is immersed in water; the purpose is to prevent the stem from taking in air or to release any air bubbles which may have formed after picking. Even though you may have cut the stem under water, it is wise to cut it again before making the arrangement. This is the most useful of all techniques and can be used in conjunction with any other method.

Method 2: Dip the cut end of the stem in peppermint oil for a few seconds.

Method 3: Split the cut end of stem.

Method 4: Dip the cut end of the stem in salt.

Method 5: Cut the stems on the slant and immerse them in boiling water. The flowers should be protected from the hot steam by a cloth or plastic bag. Do not leave flowers in the water for more than two minutes.

Method 6: Woody stems need to be crushed to enable them to absorb as much water as possible. Gentle tapping with a small hammer will split the fibres.

Method 7: Using a small syringe, inject water into stems and leaves.

Method 8: Dip the cut end of the stem into tincture of capsicum for five seconds.

Method 9: Break the stem rather than cut it.

Method 10: This is for plants which give off a milky sap. Char the cut end of the stems in a flame to seal the ends and prevent the sap from escaping. Protect the flowers with a damp cloth.

Method 11: Stand the cut end of the stem in vinegar for a few seconds.

Method 12: Dip the cut end of the stem in alcohol.

Method 13: Dip the cut end of the stem in alum.

When using any of the chemicals mentioned, cut the stems under water, then dry them before making the application of the chemical. Only use chemicals on really healthy plants. If more than one method is suggested try all of them — but not in conjunction — you may find one more effective than another.

A

Abelia	1
Acacia	3, 2
Agapanthus	1
Ageratum	1
Alyssum	1
Anemone	1
Anthurium	1
Arum lily	1, 7
Aster	2
Azaleas	1

B

Balsam	3, 2
Bamboo	Drill hole through centre stem to open nodes. Inject with water
Begonia	1
Bougainvillea	1
Broom	1

C

Caladium	4
Calendula	1
Californian poppy	2
Calla lily	1, 7
Camellia	Damp salt at base of stamens helps to stop flowers breaking
Campanula	1
Canna	2
Carnation	1
Cattleya	1
Celosia	1
China aster	3, 2
Chinese bellflower	6, 2
Chinese lantern	8
Christmas rose	1
Chrysanthemum	3, 2 or 10 or 5

H

Herbaceous peony _____ 10, 2
Hibiscus _____ 1
Hollyhock _____ 5, boiling saltwater
Honeysuckle _____ 2
Hyacinth _____ 1
Hydrangea _____ 6, 2 or 5, 13

I

Iris _____ 1
Ixia _____ 6, 5

J

Japanese quince _____ 3, 2
Jasmine _____ 2

K

Kale _____ 1

L

Larkspur _____ 8
Lilac _____ 1
Lotus _____ 7

M

Magnolia _____ 10
Maple _____ Spray leaves with glycerine or
sugar and water
Marguerite _____ 8
Michaelmas daisy _____ 1
Mimosa _____ 5
Morning glory _____ 4

Swirls of driftwood, loops of blackboy foliage with exotic white anthuriums, calathrea and sygnonium foliage.

Hand made pottery containers are an ideal choice for tall vertical arrangements. This one uses bronze flax with colourful nandina foliage and Australian banksia.

Trimmed and natural foliage create a cool green umbrella effect above the white figurine. Bright pink and red splashed foliage is used for colour contrast. Arranged in a large glass bowl with polished pebbles covering the needleholders.

Yellow and black create a striking colour combination in a shallow black bowl. Two tall yellow gladiolus give height to the clusters of golden daffodils. The black bowl is linked to the arrangement by palm foliage and blackboy loops.

PRESERVING FLOWERS

Grasses, weeds, seed-pods, everlastings, straw flowers, celosia, golden rod, acacia, yarrow and gypsophilia are all easily dried by tying in bunches and hanging upside down in a dry place. They retain their velvety texture and last well.

Another method is to pick the flowers late in the day when all moisture has gone and carefully remove all excess foliage from the stems before, even more carefully, taking the flower heads from the stems. Then put flowers and stems to dry in separate boxes containing a mixture of two parts borax to 10 parts of white cornmeal. In about two weeks, after checking to make certain they are completely dry, glue the flowers to their stalks. If the stems are hollow, insert a fine wire into them to give them strength. Flowers that have lost too much colour can be retinted with florist's flower dye. I have used sand as a drying agent quite successfully. Ingredients for sand-drying are: fine white sand; bi-carbonate of soda; silica gel (from chemist shop); paraffin wax. It is important to use only the fine white sand used by plasterers. River sand is too coarse and the sharp edges damage the soft blooms. Wash the sand several times to remove all rough pieces, twigs and foreign materials. Fill a three-quarters-full bucket of sand to the top with warm water. Stir, and if sand absorbs most of the water, add more. Do this several times then add water in which one tablespoon of detergent has been dissolved. Let the suds cover every particle of sand. Rinse several times with clear water, then dry it either by spreading it out in the sun or by heating in an oven at 250°C in a large shallow baking dish. It will take several hours to dry and will need to be stirred and turned occasionally. When the sand is dry, sift it through a fairly coarse strainer to remove any lumps.

Measure 7 kg of dry, washed sand and place in a warm oven until it is heated. Remove and add three tablespoons of melted paraffin wax. Stir until all sand has been coated. Leave to cool then add one tablespoon of bicarbonate of soda and one of powdered silica gel. Mix until all ingredients have been evenly distributed. The sharp sand is now coated and will not damage the petals.

Flower heads and stalks are dried separately. Cut flower heads from the stalks leaving 1 cm with which to hold the bloom. Strip off any excess foliage that would be below the vase rim.

Each flower head should be dried in a box deep enough to allow it to have 2 cm sand above and below it. Shoe boxes with lids are ideal. Place a 2 cm layer of sand in the box, position the flower, taking care to keep the petals intact, and gently cover with sand. Put on the lid and leave box covered for two to four weeks. After this time remove flower carefully and brush away all sand with a camel hair brush. Glue stems in place — you will have to wire hollow-centred stems. Arrange the flowers as you would fresh ones.

Preserved flowers always have to be treated gently and should never be exposed to wind or full sun. If the flower shows signs of falling apart, it will help to use a little glue at the back of the petals to hold them together.

PRESERVING FOLIAGE

Only mature foliage should be used otherwise the results could be unsatisfactory. Stand the branches in a mixture of one-third glycerine to two-thirds hot water; the heat enables the plant to absorb the mixture easily and the process will be hastened if the mixture is reheated each subsequent day.

The branches may be removed after about five or six days, but if you want the leaves to turn a really dark brown colour it is best to leave them in the mixture for about two weeks. The branches should be left hanging upside down for a time to make sure the glycerine reaches the tips of the leaves.

You can use the same method for preserving leaves on the stalk rather than as part of the branch. These leaves, because they are thinner and less heavy, will not take so much time for the glycerine to permeate them.

BLEACHING AND DYEING FLOWERS AND FOLIAGE

Some flowers and foliage not only dry well but can be bleached and used in permanent arrangements. Wisteria and grape vine can be bleached white or dyed a chosen colour. The stems must be peeled before the bleaching process begins.

First of all hang stems, cut end upwards, to dry for 10 to 14 days. When they are completely dry put a mixture of one cup of bleach to 11 L of water in a deep container and submerge the dried stems and leaves. Leave them to soak for 14 days. For the next two days rinse them thoroughly in clear water, then hang them in the sun to dry. Leave bleached, or dye with florist's dye as directed on the package. This method is only suitable for strong foliage. Tender leaves need the glycerine treatment.

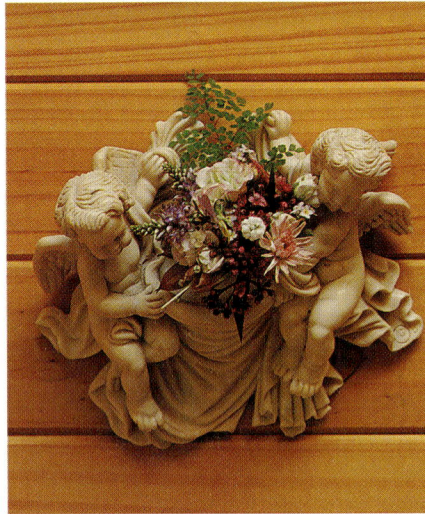

CHAPTER FOUR

CONTAINERS AND BASES

CONTAINERS

Once you become fascinated by floral art and begin to experiment with designs and materials you will find your cupboards and shelves becoming filled with an array of "finds" as the delightful mania of collecting takes over. While department stores, florists and gift shops will supply all the vases and bowls you need in the basic shapes, the fun lies in finding the unusual and unique ones. Antique shops, fetes and markets, and garage sales are all good sources of unusual containers. Antique shops which specialise in doll's houses and furniture and odd pieces of memorabilia

can provide tiny objects which are perfect for miniature arrangements. Almost anything can be used as a container to hold flowers providing it can hold water or the opening is large enough to allow the insertion of a piece of water-soaked oasis. Woolsheds, boatyards, builder's yards, town tips, kitchen pantries and the dusty back of cupboards are treasure troves; you will find things there that, no matter what their original use might have been, can be

Above: A small posy of roses and daisies in a wall vase. Opposite: An arrangement of pink flowers in an antique Venetian glass bowl is reflected in the glass of the dressing-table mirror and the mirrored base on which it stands.

just what you want to highlight an arrangement.

Do not neglect hardware shops, particularly the plumber's supply department; you will find hollow bricks, water-pipes, spiral or curved pieces of metal and lead and copper which can be beaten into just the shape you need. And if you come across a farm-plough disc, paint it black and use it on the top of a small pot to make a good-looking modern container. One of my "finds" to make an arrangement suitable for a child's room was the "spider" from a well-pump shaft.

As a collector of minerals and crystals I like to use lumps of amethyst or geodes among the flowers to coordinate with their colour.

If you can pot, do woodwork or weld metal scraps together you can make your own imaginative containers very cheaply. Factory or gift-shop "seconds" are another cheap source of supply. So are baskets. Porous ceramic containers can be made waterproof by the application of several coats of lacquer or water-glass, and if you use water-soaked oasis wrapped in aluminium foil, water should not drip out of a basket.

A turned baluster or piece of stair-rail will make a tall and graceful container if you set a cup-holder in the top and secure it to a flat wooden base. Small tin cans which once contained jam, fruit or fish can be painted black and used with a needle-holder or a piece of soaked oasis tucked inside. You can paint them any colour you wish, of course, but, on the whole, using flat black paint is most successful as the colour does not detract from the flowers. A tall cylindrical can covered with black velvet Contact looks very elegant. You can even solder several juice cans together to make interesting shapes. It is wise to pour sand into containers of this type to prevent them becoming top-heavy. A spaghetti jar also makes a good tall container.

Another way of creating a tall arrangement is to use a piece of driftwood with a cup-holder screwed into it. The driftwood should be firmly secured to a base. You can have a lamp today and a flower container tomorrow by changing the lamp fitting in a lamp base to a screw-in cup-holder; nothing is sacred in floral art! Trophies, family heirlooms, delicate porcelain figurines, silver bowls, silver candlesticks, so often destined to remain in the cupboard, can be brought out and really enjoyed as they give a special style and elegance to your floral designs.

Some family heirlooms are more difficult to use, however. The heavily decorated hand-painted china vases, popular in the Victorian era, are so covered with floral motifs that they distract the eye from the flowers. This type of vase is best used only for formal massed arrangements — here the profusion of flowers and the weight of their colours may enable the arrangement to hold its own. Heavily cut-crystal vases can also be a problem for they allow the flower stalks and the mechanics of the arrangement to be seen. You can dye the water with food colouring or add milk to it, but, on the whole, I prefer not to use them. There are, of course, many glass containers that are perfect to use; the

Japanese ikebana frosted vases are superb, and Bristol blue, and ruby glass vases and vaseline glass look delightful with well-chosen flowers.

BASES

The base on which an arrangement stands is a very important part of floral art. It should be solid but not so heavy it cannot be moved easily, and should be of a material suitable for the position in which the arrangement is to stand, which could be on a table, floor, mantelpiece, etc. Choose between timber, glass, metal, stone and bamboo. Felt pads should be fastened to the bottom of any base which is to stand on polished wood. Although a base will usually protect furniture from damage by moisture, care should be taken at all times.

The shape of a base will determine the design of the arrangement to accompany it. You can arrange figurines, pieces of driftwood, fruit or any pretty little thing against a background of flowers held in a plastic container, skilfully hidden, in many different ways and can make alterations easily without disturbing the basic design.

WOODEN BASES

You can make wooden bases from pieces of wood with the bark intact from as small as 6 cm in diameter for miniature arrangements to really large ones for floor arrangements. The cut can be made straight or diagonally. Most woods are suitable but it is advisable to let the pieces dry out thoroughly before you use them or you could find that they will crack while in use. You can varnish the wood, if you prefer a polished look, but if you like the natural look, just varnish the underside. Slats of polished wood about 30 cm long and 8 cm wide, used either singly or together, make excellent bases. Black wooden bases, some with small legs, are available in different sizes and shapes, and are particularly effective when used with an oriental type of arrangement.

SLATE AND STONE BASES

The lovely grading of colour found in slate and stone makes these two materials very useful for making into bases; they can be used as tiles or cut into irregular shapes. The glitter of mica in a piece of stone can blend with the colour of the flowers used in the arrangement.

DRIFTWOOD AND BARK BASES

You may find a piece of driftwood or bark which will stand steadily enough to make a base, otherwise you can glue a piece to a base made from another material and make it an integral part of the base. It is possible to tie the driftwood into place but bark, which is more brittle, will need glueing.

MIRROR-GLASS BASES

Nothing is more effective than a mirror-glass base for an arrangement of flowers for a dining-table. The reflection of flowers and candlelight in the sparkling glass can be magical. Particular attention must be paid to the balance of the arrangement for

Top: A collection of tiny vases about the size of an Australian golden dollar — which is also displayed. The base on which they sit is a redwood burl from California. Above: Bamboo laced together with leather thonging to make a base for an arrangement of white daisies and wheat in a blue-and-white Japanese teapot.

Top: Set on a cream glass base the Royal Doulton figurine provides a romantic evening dance theme. The curving fern gives movement to the cream roses and columbines. Above: A stone base sets the colour theme for this naturalistic arrangement of pink carnations, columbines and deep purple *brunsfelsia calcina*.

A serene white-figurine stands beside pale pink peony roses arranged in a long white bowl.

the flowers' mirror image will of course double the effect. I like to use mirror-glass for arrangements on my dressing-table. Mirror-glass can be cut into ovals, circles, oblongs or squares; the different sizes can be mixed or matched. Always ask the glazier to polish the edges of any glass cut for you as they are sharp and can inflict some nasty cuts. If you cut your own glass always bind the edges with narrow invisible tape.

You can change the colour of a silver mirror base by placing a thin sheet of coloured glass, either plain or impressed, over it. Strips of coloured glass edging a clear mirror look very attractive, and silver mirror, bordered by opaque black glass, looks stunning used with modern arrangements of exotic flowers like orchids and anthuriums. I use mirrors of royal blue, silver, gold, rosy pink and charcoal and contrast or blend the shades. A small handbag mirror, or one taken from a powder compact, makes a good base for a miniature arrangement.

PLATE-GLASS BASES

The glass can be cut into ovals, circles, squares, etc, and the pieces can be used overlapped or built up using cup-holders or the tops or aerosol cans as separators. Black plate glass used as a base for an all-white arrangement of flowers, or black-and-white plate glass used with scarlet flowers can make a modern or abstract arrangement look highly dramatic.

MARBLE AND ONYX BASES

You find onyx in lovely shades of green and brown; marble comes in many different shades. One of the best places to find marble is the bathroom-supply store; the pieces cut from a sheet of marble to allow the insertion of the washbasin are just the size you need. It is easy to glue a container to bases of this sort if you are anxious about the stability of an arrangement.

BAMBOO AND CANE BASES

Lengths of bamboo, from the thickness of a pencil to much larger sizes, can be laced together with leather thonging to make a base. The bamboo can be stained and lacquered if you wish, and mats of different sizes can be joined together to make any size you need. You can do your own canework and have mats of any size or shape. If you do not want to make your own there are plenty of ready-made bamboo and cane ones available.

FLORAL PICTURES

A shadow box framed as a picture can make an excellent container for a floral arrangement.

The boxes can be of any size from small ones suitable for a bedroom or loungeroom to very large ones ideal for foyers and large hallways.

The larger frames can stand on an easel, while smaller ones can hang on the wall. Antique picture frames are ideal.

The shadow box only needs to be 8 to 10cms deep and can be framed to match paintings in the home.

After selecting the shadow box,

choose a small flower holder of appropriate size and cut it in half. Glue it to the back of the shadow box with the uncut side facing outwards. Fill the holder with an oasis and arrange flowers.

This is a very attractive way to make a 'living' floral picture. Dried flowers can be used instead of fresh flowers.

CHAPTER FIVE

DESIGN PRINCIPLES AND MATERIALS

DESIGN

A really successful arrangement does not look contrived — this takes away from even the most beautiful flowers. You do not need masses of flowers of different shapes and colours, in fact it is often an advantage to be short of material, for then you become aware of the potential of each piece and will take pains to use it to the best advantage.

The design should suit the position where the arrangement is to stand. Look at the background walls, furniture and sur-rounding space before you decide what to do. The shape and site of the arrangement will be determined by what you see.

Basic designs are simple and the guidelines and rules will help you master them quickly. You will then be able to experiment with ideas of your own. First you must create the frame or outline of the design. Once the outline has been formed

Above: Purple Patterson's curse flower spikes and five pale pink roses in a Belleek vase with antique shaving mugs all link the colours of a country bathroom. Opposite: Phaelenopsis and pink erica in a silver coffee-pot highlight the bright pink of the dress of the figurine.

it will be easy to finish it with the flowers or foliage you have available. All arrangements must be stable; there is little point in creating a beautiful effect that will be ruined if it topples over or is moved, so make full use of needle-holders and oasis to hold everything in place.

Traditional arrangements, handed down through generations were described in simple geometric terms; circles, arcs, S curves, triangles, ovals, stars and mass, and were symmetrical or asymmetrical. Flowers and foliage were grown in abundance in the large gardens and estates and large massed arrangements were in keeping with the furniture of the period.

Today floral art calls for designs with sharp, clean outlines, created quickly and using few flowers. A quick, pleasing design can be created by using a lovely branch with just one or two special flowers as a focal point. A branch of tortured willow, well placed or flowering cherry, crab apple, pear, peach or prunus with a full-blown rose, peony or chrysanthemum is all that is needed to make a dramatic design.

THE VERTICAL LINE

This arrangement should be tall, slender, streamlined and uncluttered. Flowers or foliage should lead the eye upwards from the centre of the container, which has one focal point of interest at the base. The height of the arrangement should not be less than one and a half times the height of an upright container and taller if light and airy materials are used.

If you use a shallow rectangular or round bowl the height of the materials should be twice the width of the container. If the container is placed on a base, include the width of the base in your calculation. Failing to do this could make the arrangement look squat and dumpy and the vertical effect would be lost. In this graceful, elegant arrangement all stems must emerge from one point.

Needle-holders must be secured in the centre of the container which should be heavy enough to balance the weight of the tall-stemmed materials. Guidelines and rules say that, if arranged in a shallow container, the flowers and foliage may come to, but not extend over, the rim. In an upright container the widest part of the arrangement should not extend further than one-quarter of the width of the container on either side (for example, an arrangement in an 8 cm wide container must not exceed 12 cms in width). Everything must be kept in proportion. It is better to use needle-holders with a heavy base than oasis in this type of design.

Use tall, straight foliage or flowers for the main central axis with other leaves or flowers, closely placed and graduated in height, to support the main line. To give interest to the focal area at the base, use two clusters of foliage, of different shape than that of the main stems, as a background to some lovely rounded blooms at the point of emergence. But be careful not to use too much material . . . keep the tall, uncluttered vertical line.

This arrangement is ideal for narrow areas, hallways, side tables and buffets where table space is required. Flax, gladiolus, sansevieria and iris foliage look lovely as the outline of the design with aralia, maple foliage, roses, peonies or chrysanthemums used as the focal point of interest.

Curved pussy pillow, scarlet cattleya orchids and phaelenopsis arranged in a low glass bowl and reflected in the modern mirrored lamp base.

An antique silver fruit bowl filled with white candytuft and phaelenopsis set in an oasis.

THE HORIZONTAL DESIGN

For a long, narrow arrangement on a buffet table the horizontal design can be used with a low bowl or a tall container such as a candlestick. The arrangement should be one and a half times the height of the tall upright container or twice as wide, or even wider than a low bowl for a table arrangement. Oasis is ideal for securing stalks into position. Stiff-stemmed flowers and foliage will keep the horizontal effect and should be graduated in length. The centre of the design should form a rounded mound with the point of interest in the centre. Use foliage to form the outline and fill the centre with special flowers. The flower leaves should cover the edge of the container but do not use drooping, curving foliage which would take away from the horizontal line.

For a really modern effect a low horizontal arrangement in a shallow bowl can have three or four straight leaves pointed on one side of the arrangement with only stalks to balance the other side. Streletzia is ideal for this. Exotic anthuriums can be placed in the centre.

An arrangement with a ''formal'' balance has an equal distribution of visual weight either side of the central point. ''Informal'' balance makes an interesting arrangement with fine, delicate flowers on one side of the central axis and larger, strong-coloured blooms on the other. Colour can be used for a dramatic effect. If an arrangement has to be viewed from both sides then make them both equally attractive.

THE FAN DESIGN

We all know the shape of an opened fan. An arrangement of flowers must convey they rhythmic loveliness of a fan being gently swept from side to side. The container can be low and flat or can have a narrowed base which suggests the handles of a fan. You will need a piece of oasis to hold the flowers in place. The centre stem should be one and a half times the height of the container above the rim; the others, each one a little shorter, should be arranged, in equal number, on each side of the centre stem, dwindling away both in size and colour towards the outside flowers. The flowers should all rise from the same central position. Arrange the back row first; their stems can be hidden, but only subtly by flowers of the same sort with short stems, placed in front in a similar fan shape.

For fun you can add a lace frill and silk handle. The frill is easily placed at the top

or bottom using florist's wire. The fan design makes a pretty centrepiece for a bridal shower or birthday party for an older person. Arrange it in a champagne glass held by a white glove with jewelled bracelet cuff. This one me a champion ribbon at a flower show.

THE TRIANGULAR DESIGN

This is the most popular design of all; the triangle can be symmetrical or assymmetrical, and it will always look good. You can vary the shape by altering the degree of angle of the sides, so that the design can be vertical or horizontal. You can use containers of any size and still achieve a good effect. The design lends itself to both traditional and modern arrangements.

If you use a small, low container, place your needle-holder or oasis either in the middle of it or to one side, depending on your choice of design.

Remeber the basic principle — to achieve unity of the design, all the material must emerge from the same point.

THE DIAGONAL DESIGN

This arrangement is useful when you have only a few flowers. It is easier to arrange in a full container. Oasis will be needed to keep the flowers in place. A vase with side openings may be useful. Keep the line graceful and arrange the material so that it looks attractive on both sides if it is placed on a table or against a mirror.

A rose in a sterling-silver yachting trophy adds a finishing touch to this dressing table.

A still-life basket arrangement of mixed flowers (daffoldils, carnations and calendulas) add colour to any spot in a home.

THE OVAL DESIGN

Used vertically, an oval arrangement makes a graceful display for a coffee table or mantelpiece; used horizontally, it is an attractive asymmetrical design for a dinner table.

The flowers should be arranged in a low bowl and held in place by needle-holders or oasis crossed with chicken wire pegged into position. The line can be created by using the technique for curving branches described in Chapter 7. Pussywillow has beautifully pliable stems. Always use sparsely leaved stems to keep the uncluttered line. Fill in the centre of the design with flowers or foliage and cover the rim of the bowl.

Pussywillow with roses in bud, half-opened and in full bloom look lovely. The Pussywillow lasts well and the roses in the central focus area can easily be replaced when they fade.

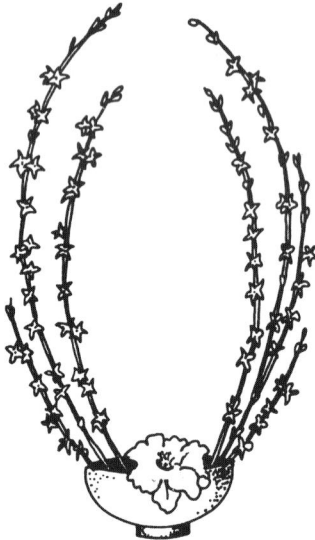

THE CIRCULAR DESIGN

A round design needs a round container; everything must contribute to the self-contained line.

Short-stemmed flower heads, all of the same colour, can be used in graduated size with the largest bloom in the centre, or you can use contrast with the colour wheel as a guide for outstanding effect. Try blue against orange with pure white for an informal luncheon outdoors, or place candles in the centre. Edge the bowl with foliage. Whatever flowers or foliage you use, keep the circle shape and form a raised mound in the centre.

THE CRESCENT DESIGN

This graceful design suits traditional homes with antique furniture and can be used with low or tall containers. It looks attractive in a tall candlestick or a comport on legs.

Graduated stems form the shape of a newly risen moon that can be tilted to whatever angle you please. The main stems almost complete a three-quarter circle but must be closely backed by curved graduated-length stems.

Crab apple, willow, prunus, cherry flowers, peach and yellow broom stems are easily bent and curved into this design. Flowers at the low focal point can be from one bud to full bloom, with a group of three larger rounded shapes at the main point of interest. Form the crescent with one line of flowers such as tulips or rose buds, with dainty, fine filler that adds to the design, giving it a lighter effect.

THE HOGARTH DESIGN

This design has lots of movement. It is similar to the crescent in construction but the curves go in opposite directions like a curving S bend. The two half-moons face in opposite directions and create a beautiful flowing line.

Form the outline with uncluttered foliage to give that carefree effect. Use oasis for holding the stems in place and anchor it tightly to the top of the candlestick or tall container. The Hogarth line makes an elegant arrangement in a tall container or an interesting design with horizontal curves for a shallow bowl for the centre of a dining-table.

MATERIALS

USING NATURAL MATERIALS

Driftwood
Sculptured by sand, wind and time, no two shapes of it are ever the same, and driftwood is a joy to use. Flowers look particularly soft and lovely when displayed against the old weathered wood and you can always find a piece to give height and line to an arrangement, or solidity and repose if your design is to be horizontal. Only the imagination limits the use of driftwood. It can stand on its own or be secured to a heavy base for eas eof handling. It can represent a tree or a mountain in a creative design; it can be stained and polished and used with tulips, roses or Hawaiian hibiscus in a particularly lovely combination. If you use driftwood, though, be certain to keep the design simple and uncluttered. The beauty of the arrangement should be in the line.

Cup-holders and orchid tubes are useful for holding the flowers, as they are small enough to be hidden and placed at whatever height you desire by the skilful use of ties or wire. They are particularly good for use in a permanent arrangement as the flowers can easily be replaced as they fade.

Tree roots and stones also have their place; a gnarled misshapen hunk of root or a large coloured piece of stone, smoothed by water, can give interest to an otherwise ordinary handful of flowers and leaves.

This miniature arrangement on a base of pine gains significance by contrasting delicacy with heaviness and bulk.

Florist's clay can be used to hold the components in place.

Bark
You can find pieces of bark in any park or bushland. Use it to make long, curling strips to add to an arrangement. Geraniums, carnations, daisies and roses look particularly lovely with the textured brown "curls".

The container is one of the first pieces of pottery I ever made — I like to think its unevenness gives it added charm. The wood gives height to the arrangement while the cream glass base mellows it. The three golden roses can be replaced as they fade.

Dried flowers and leaves

Dried material naturally does not need water and can be inserted in dry oasis in a container, or wired and taped into position in an arrangement. Its advantage is that it will not flop or fade so that the arrangement can be at least semi-permanent. The wonderful brown tones of foliage dried by the glycerine method (see p. 25) look very handsome with the bright colours of everlasting flowers. Fresh flowers can be arranged in water with dried foliage as a background.

Foliage

The varied colours and shapes of foliage make it possible to make lovely arrangements featuring leaves only. You can blend or contrast them; designs can range from the quietly harmonious to the dramatic and striking. A cluster of coloured leaves will make a focal point at the base of a tall or spreading arrangement.

Flowering pot plants

Orchids in pots are long-lasting, especially during the hot summer months. Floor arrangements can be attractive featuring orchids teamed with driftwood. Any potted plant in flower can be incorporated into an arrangement but the pot must be hidden. A permanent arrangement using driftwood and dried material can be transformed just by changing the potted plant.

Fruit

Fruit is particulary suitable for arrangements for the breakfast table or for outdoor dining. Apples, kumquats, mandarins, bunches of cherries, etc., can be wired to a piece of bamboo or thick sections of branch of varying size. Grapes also look attractive spilling over the edge of a formal arrangement.

MIRROR MAGIC

The beauty of flowers reflected in a silvery mirror can take one's breath away but the arrangement must be carefully executed. If you have an arrangement standing in front of a mirror, care must be taken to ensure that the back of it is as attractive as the front, for it will be seen all round. If an arrangement is reflected in a mirror base, there should be economy of line for everything will be seen twice.

USING FIGURINES

One of the loveliest ways of displaying a cherished figurine is very simple. Attach a small cup-holder firmly to the top of a brass rod or wooden dowel, then glue the rod or dowel securely near the back of your chosen base. You can then place the figurine in front of the base and choose flowers for the cup-holder to make a background. You can change flowers and figurine as you wish. You can buy brass rods with threaded ends which enable a cup-holder to be screwed on to it.

The figurines should not overpower an arrangement but simply add something to it. They should be only about one-third the height of the arrangement and should be placed so that they are looking into the arrangement. Pretty figurines look best with delicate flowers the colour of the glaze of the porcelain. Wooden figurines, particularly oriental ones, need something more exotic such as orchids, anthuriums and palm leaves.

PAINTINGS

A striking still-life painting will seem even more striking if you use it as background to an exact reproduction of itself together with flowers that echo the colours used. A seascape can be combined with an arrangement incorporating material gathered from the beach. An abstract painting can be linked with a modern arrangement that uses the same line and colour. A large picture frame can be used to turn an arrangement into a "picture".

USING LIGHTING

Modern decor calls for clear-cut, often dramatic arrangements. The use of low voltage halogen lighting to spotlight flower arrangements has become very popular as the brilliant white light accentuates and enriches the colours. Ceiling spotlights have a built in transformer which combines with other types of lighting.

SAYING "WELCOME"

A lovely tradition I would like to see revived is the "welcome" vase. A wall-vase, filled with fragrant flowers, is surely one of the nicest ways of welcoming guests as they arrive. The vase should be placed high enough to be out of the reach of children but near the eye-level of anyone who is standing waiting at your door. Any container that can lie flat against the wall will suffice and baskets are attractive. The container need not hold water as the flowers can be placed in oasis.

USING TINY TREASURES

The miniature arrangement is the darling of many of us in the floral-art world. There is such fun in searching for the delicate, tiny object which can be teamed with the even tinier flowers with small faces and slender stems. Pill-boxes, shells, crystal geodes, small copper replicas of saucepans, etc., the fragile cups of toy tea-sets once beloved by children — the list is endless. The great art in making a really successful miniature arrangement lies in proportion and balance; everything must be to scale and no accessory should overpower another.

SETTING A THEME

Only imagination limits the use of accessories used with flowers to make a special theme come alive. I have seen harps, grand pianos and cellos used very successfully, large though they are. Most of the arrangements of this type are "fun" arrangements and the effect is bold. Yacht clubs can make use of anchors, steering wheels and all manner of ship's chandlery; golf clubs can use green flags, wooden sticks and silver trophies. Colour is important; the dominant one should be the one associated with the sport or club. Ingenuity will be needed if you are called on to make an arrangement for a rugby club dinner and are asked to incorporate the club's stuffed mascot!

There are, of course, arrangements used to suggest a mood, time or place, and these are very different. The skill and imagination of the floral artist face their greatest challenge here.

CHAPTER SIX

LIVING WITH FLOWERS

FOYERS

Large foyers need large arrangements. Floor arrangements must have impact, showing skilled use of balance and colour. Because of the inevitable draughts only hardy plants should be used. Driftwood, branches, large green-leaved plants, potted plants and fresh flowers can be used in an endless variety of combinations. The arrangements should be kept out of the line of traffic unless they are needed to ''steer'' people in a certain direction.

Pedestal arrangements should be as strikingly arranged and as colourful as possible otherwise they will become lost. Care should be taken that the material does not obtrude and brush against passers-by or invite young children to fiddle with the flowers. Water-gardens, with the arrangement in the centre, are very suitable. Flowers look lovely against the cool water which will keep them fresh.

Above: A fireplace can lose all its life when it is not in use; flowers can make all the difference. A large copper pan full of potted gerberas, vibrant with colour, bring vitality back into the room.
Right: A green and white Royal Doulton figurine looks up into an arrangement of tiny white-green roses in a vaseline glass vase, and so looks part of the arrangement.

ENTRANCE HALL

The entrance hall to a house usually contains a table that features largely in family life. Keys are thrown on it, messages are left on it, the visitor's book sits there — it is also a very good place to put your second "welcome" vase.

No rules apply to arrangements for a hall so you can let yourself go and have fun. In summer why not try a winter arrangement to make a hot day feel less oppressive? Pale flowers, bare branches, a scattering of Epsom salts or shattered windscreen glass, or a container of cold, sharp blue. A large pale-green dish, filled with water on which flower heads float, with lumps of jade, crystal or sparkling amethyst will look clean and cool as accessories. In winter you can bring back the warmth of summer by using an arrangement of orange and yellow flowers.

I used to enjoy leaving "cryptic" arrangements on the hall table so that my family could figure out what I had been doing during the day. It takes ingenuity to say "I have been shopping" in flowers!

DINING-ROOMS

A formal dining party gives you the opportunity to bring out the silver candelabra and your finest china and to make a classic "formal" arrangement. A golden rule is never to use highly perfumed flowers; nothing should compete with the aroma of the food. Another rule is never make the arrangement more than 30 cm high or you guests will be unable to talk to each other across the table without bobbing and weaving about in their chairs.

If you have a round table your arrangement should go in the centre of it; if the table is long or oblong you can use more than one arrangement. If you use candles or candelabra — and what is a formal party without the magic of candles? — keep the arrangement long and low.

You can also place a tiny arrangement by each guest's name-card, and, using "the language of flowers" (See Chapter 9 "Flower Talk") send a secret message to a special guest.

LOUNGEROOMS

Formal arrangements using comports, fine china and silver vases and bowls look best here. Strong dramatic arrangements, "modern" in concept, will be better suited to rooms where the general trend of taste is "modern" in that bookshelves and bookcases, etc, are made from materials other than wood, chairs are not the traditional sitting-room type and there are unframed prints rather than pictures on the walls. The mood of the flower arrangements should be in tune with the background. This is where you sit and talk with your guests and the flowers will be very much on view; a clash of colours and styles may eventually become irritating.

FAMILY ROOMS

A family room is often the most comfortable and the most used room in the house. An ornate or striking arrangement would look out of place. Clean, simple, cheerful, pretty ones have the right sort of "feel" here.

BEDROOMS

This is where pretty flowers and pretty containers come into their own. Roses, gardenias, lavender, carnations, forget-me-nots and fragrant hyacinths are lovely bedroom flowers. I have a desk in my bedroom where I love to sit and write with the perfume of roses around me.

A small arrangement on the bedside table, another one on the dressing-table where the flowers can be reflected in the mirror for the adults. Attractive mobiles and pretty arrangements in dainty containers or pots of cheerful flowers among the mementoes are arrangements children love and they make the bedroom an inviting place.

BATHROOMS AND POWDER-ROOMS

I like to use small, fine china vases and fragrant, pretty flowers in the bathroom. A large pink shell is one of my favourite containers. Shells, packed with water-soaked oasis and used with a simple arrangement of only a few flowers look just right. A taller arrangement reflected in the mirror of a vanity unit gives an added touch of luxury.

KITCHENS

Flowers in the kitchen can give the cook a much-needed splash of colour. Roadside flowers and grasses, garden flowers, potted plants all add gaiety and colour. You can use mustard pots, bottles, handmade pottery, earthenware jugs, Dutch clogs, cane baskets, copper saucepans and kettles, teapots and many other "finds" — as containers. If you use a teapot place the lid close by to complete the arrangement.

THE BREAKFAST TABLE

Flowers for a breakfast table should be bright and gay but not heavily perfumed. I grow special "cottage-garden" flowers to greet us in the mornings. If the breakfast is taken in the kitchen the containers used for the table can be kitchen ones, as mentioned above; if breakfast is taken in another room in the house it is nicer to use bowls and vases which have a less utilitarian look. The colours used at breakfast time, for both flowers and containers, should be clean and fresh. Blue and white is a particularly pleasing combination. I once used a Dutch clog filled with tulips to greet my guests with their bacon and eggs and they loved it.

OFFICES

An office needs flowers if it is not to have that soulless look. It is not enough to be super-efficient — clients like to feel their bank managers or solicitors have a heart too.

Traditional arrangements do not look right here. The best ones to use are "modern" ones with clean lines and the

An arrangement for a formal dinner party. The flowers do not obstruct conversation across the table.

Bringing the garden into the room! The emptiness of the fireplace is hidden by pots of gloxinias, gerberas, spathiphyllum, calatheas and bronze foliage.

flowers should be the freshest and of the best quality obtainable. A high quality but not ostentatious effect is one to aim for.

An arrangement in a large, low bowl with only a few flowers, a piece of rock or mineral or very large, smooth pebble, and clear, undisturbed water which will pick up the light will create a relaxed atmosphere.

The angular corners of the room can be softened by tall plants with well-defined leaves. the ''cosy'' or the ''quaint'' look has no place in an office; fussiness in an arrangement is always to be avoided and it would look particularly out of place here.

ARRANGEMENTS FOR MEAL-TIMES

BUFFETS

The food is usually the main attraction when a buffet meal is well set out but you can excite the tastebuds even further by delighting the eye too. Create a vision of plenty by filling your largest silver pieces with fruit and flowers or use a cane basket to make a magnificent cornucopia, rich in colour and overflowing.

Your arrangements should complement, not overpower the interest created by the presentation of the food. If the meal is a simple one, use the simple country flowers with grasses and wheat. If it is more sophisticated, use exotic flowers such as orchids or anthuriums to create the mood.

Accessories can be unusual but always

in keeping with the type of food being presented. I once used some stuffed pheasants to great effect.

LUNCHEONS

Indoor lunches for friends give you the chance to be a bit of a show-off if the mood takes you — it is always enjoyable to impress one's peers! If you are feeling grand, here is the chance to use fine china and crystal with the loveliest flowers you can find; if you are feeling inventive use the oval, the fan or the Hogarth curve as your design to show your skill at its best. Of course a simple lunch taken in the kitchen or the family room is something else and an arrangement with clean simple lines is best here.

PATIO MEALS

Since these are informal the flower arrangements should be simple, although it is still possible to achieve an unusual effect. A round loaf of bread, hollowed out, makes an unexpected container for wheat stalks and daisies. Pineapple and coconut halves, clam shells, large seashells and copper cookware can all be pressed into service as containers. We do a lot of outdoor entertaining for guests from overseas and I decorate the tables with flags of the nation of our guests with flower arrangements done in the national colours — yellow and blue for Swedish guest; red, white and blue for the English, etc.

A meal taken on the patio at night can have the extra glamour of candles if you use glass-lamp chimneys to prevent them blowing out.

SEAFOOD MEALS

You can create the right atmosphere by making a "seascape" arrangement, using pieces of fishing-net, coral, the shells of lobster and crab, sea shells, etc., with palm leaves and the flowers of the hibiscus and frangipani.

CHAPTER SEVEN

FLORAL-ART HINTS

To enable the cut stems of flowers and branches to fit into a needle-holder easily, cut them to a point. Split tough branch stems into four.

To insert flowers into oasis without damage, first make the holes with a skewer or thin pencil.

To hold flower stems in position in a tall container, take two pieces of branch a fraction longer than the width of the mouth of the container, criss-cross them and then jam them tightly into the container.

If a branch in an arrangement is unsteady, support it by a small forked crutch made from a twig.

To curve and bend stems without snapping them, place thumbs underneath the place on the stem where you require the curve, apply pressure and gently bend the stem.

If a flower stem or branch cannot stand up by itself in the needle-holder, wedge it into position with a short piece of stem cut from another plant or tape it to the stem.

Above: Inserting a stem in a needle-holder at the required angle.

Top: A carnation with a short stem inserted into an orchid tube that is strapped to a tall cane stake so that the flower can take its place at the top of a tall arrangement. Above: A flower stem taped to a short piece of stronger stem to enable it to be held in position.

Top: A stem held in position in a large container by the use of small pieces of branch. Above: Making a hole in oasis to enable the flower stem to be inserted without damage.

Insert florist's wire or a thin bamboo stick down the hollow stem of a flower that could not otherwise hold its position.

Flowers with stems too thin to enable them to stand up by themselves in the needle-holder need help. Cut about 2 cm lengths of stem from hollow-stemmed flowers such as zinnias or dahlias, insert the thin stems in the short, hollow pieces and arrange in the needle-holder. The thin-stemmed flowers will be able to take up all the water they need.

If flowers are required to lie horizontally, cushion and support them by placing 3 cm lengths of stem across the needle-holder.

If blooms in the middle of an arrangement begin to droop and need replacing, do not pull them out as you could disturb the whole arrangement. Instead, cut of the stem just below the level of the adjacent flowers, and gently insert a replacement in the original position.

Misting finished arrangements will keep them fresh and dewy-looking.

Orchid tubes or pill tubes can be taped to bamboo sticks and used if a short-stemmed flower is needed at the top of an arrangement. The tubes can be hidden behind the flowers and foliage.

Poppies and other single stemmed flowers present a challenge as they can look very ordinary if a bunch of them is just placed in a container. Try tying three or four flowers together so that they look like a rhododendron flower. Group the pastel-shaded ones together.

Use flowers from bud to full bloom in the same arrangement to create interest and variety.

Place flowers of the same type together; do not scatter them through the arrangement or you could get a "patchy" effect.

When cutting flowers cut the stems longer than they will be in the vase so that, when they are cut under water before you make the arrangement, they will be the correct height.

Do not arrange flowers at all the same height. If the bunch you buy has stems of equal length insert them in pieces of hollow stem to cut to unequal lengths and then arrange them.

Create space. Leaving out a flower will do more for an arrangement than if you include extra ones just because you have them.

Unless especially needed for an effect in abstract or modern arrangements, do not arrange flowers and leaves so that they are all facing the same way.

Use the deepest shades you have at the bottom of an arrangement of pastel-coloured flowers.

If the only roses available are all at the same

stage of development, remove the outer petals of some of the flowers so that they look more like buds.

Accessories like figurines should be placed so that they face into the arrangement and so look part of it.

Chrysanthemums take up water better if the stems are snapped instead of being cut.

Flowers with sappy stems such as lilies, daffodils, tulips and bluebells should not be given the hot water treatment. Just cut 1.5 cm off the cut end of the stem each day while they are waiting to be arranged.

To help hollow-stemmed flowers to last longer, hold the stem with the cut end upwards and trickle water into it until the stem is full. Keep your finger on the cut end and only release it when the stem is immersed in water.

To prevent maple leaves from curling, stand the stems in a mixture of glycerine and water.

To prevent ornamental grasses wilting, stand them in vinegar and water.

Day lilies needed for an arrangement for an evening party should be cut in the morning while they are closed and kept in the refrigerator for the rest of the day. When brought out for the evening they will stay open for about eight hours under electric light.

Waterlilies will last longer if the injection into the leaves and stems is a mixture of three parts water to one part alcohol.

CHAPTER EIGHT

FLOWER SHOWS

A clear understanding of the terms used in floral art is necessary if an exhibitor is to be able to interpret the requirements of flower show judges correctly. The simple definitions given below are generally considered acceptable. Some of them are taken from the Victorian Judges School for Floral Art handbook. Flower shows generally issue copies of their schedule which detail the requirements for entry, etc.

ABSTRACT. An expression composed of line, form, colour and strongly contrasted texture. Attention is focused on the entire composition, the designer taking what is felt to be the essence of the material and trying to communicate it to the observer. The arrangement may be expressive, in that the organisation of all elements expresses an idea or theme, or non-objective in that it creates an awareness of the material as pure form.

Above: A discarded "spider" from a farm bore, painted black and with a single stem of bromeliad emerging from it, gives the effect of a rocket taking off into space. It is set on overlapping glass bases of black and white. Right: A modern arrangement using river-oak roots, two superb cattleya orchids and aralia leaves. The tall handmade pottery container complements the naturalness of the roots which still have the pebbles from the river bank where they grew and contrasts quite dramatically with the flowers.

ACCENT. Emphasis (noun). To emphasise or feature (verb).

ACCESSORY. Anything added to the arrangement to complete the design.

ACHROMATIC COLOURS. Colours lacking hue and chroma — neutral colours — black, white and grey.

ADJACENT HUES. Hues lying near, or adjacent to each other on the colour wheel.

ADVANCING HUES. Warm colours, from red to yellow and their intermediate colours.

ANALAGOUS COLOURS. Colours that lie next to each other or close together on the colour wheel.

ARRANGEMENT. Creation of an effect using the principles of design.

ARTIFICIAL. Not natural.

ASSEMBLAGE. A collection of plant material and other "found" objects, which is abstract in conception. The unrelated objects are placed together and unified by colour, purpose, space and repetition. There are two types:
— a wall-hanging by itself or in conjunction with an arrangement;
— a single unit, sculptural in construction.

BACKGROUND. The background against which the arrangement is viewed.

BALANCE. Visual stability.

BASE. An article on which a container or arrangement stands. It can be of wood, metal, slate, glass, fabric, etc.

BASKET. A container with a handle with which it can be carried, hand made of any natural woven material unless otherwise specified. Two-thirds of the handle should show in the design.

Presentation basket. See Wired work.

Arranged basket. Arranged to be viewed either from the front or from all round, according to the schedule, which should also state whether a "wired" basket is required. Baskets of flowers with stems in water or water-retaining material do not come under wired work.

A basket of flowers. A basket containing flowers without any wiring or tying.

BLOOM. A single flower on a stem.

BOUQUET. A bunch of flowers which may or may not be wired, and with or without "trails". See Wired work.

BOWL. A round container wider than it is high.

BRIDAL SHEAF. See Wired work.

BUD. A bud becomes a flower when there are more than two petals unfurling from its point.

CHROMA. The degree of strength or weakness of a hue. "Full chroma" is a hue at its greatest intensity.

CHROMATIC COLOURS. All colours other than neutral ones (black, white, grey).

COLLAGE. An abstract design, mounted on a background panel, with or without a frame, created by fixing a combination of diverse, often unrelated objects to emphasise texture and three-dimensional effects.

COLOUR WHEEL. A circle of colours graded by the addition of varying amounts of black and white.

COMPOSITION. A planned design comprising plant material, container and one or more accessories.

CONDITION. The physical state of plant material.

CONTAINER. A receptacle of any shape, design or material in which plant material is exhibited.

CONTEMPORARY ARRANGEMENTS. Arrangements in keeping with modern trends.

CONTRAST. The use of opposites in colour, texture, line, form etc.

CREATIVITY. See Originality.

CRESCENT. A crescent is part of a circle. The design should widen at the central focal area; the ends should narrow to points. The ends of any ribbon used should not hang vertically from the centre as this would disturb the flow of the design.

DESIGN. The planned order of the elements used.

DESIGN ELEMENTS. These are: space, line, form, pattern, texture and colour.

DIRECTION. The movement through the arrangement and into space.

DISTINCTION. Marked superiority in all respects. Not to be confused with originality.

DOMINANCE. A design principle. The governing or controlling of a design by one of its elements.

DRIED PLANT MATERIAL. Natural material which has been dried, preserved or bleached.

DRIFTWOOD. Wood which has been weathered by any of the natural elements, that is, earth, fire, water or wind.

DYED PLANT MATERIAL. This must be used according to the schedule ruling.

EXPRESSIVE ARRANGEMENT. An arrangement which expresses or portrays an idea or theme.

FEATURE. A specific flower or accessory that is made the centre of interest. "To feature" is to give prominence to something.

FINISH. The perfection of all the elements of the arrangement.

FLORET. A small flower forming part of a multiple head.

FLOOR ARRANGEMENT. A large arrangement intended to stand at floor-level and which can be free-standing, frontal, modern or traditional in style. Containers, with or without stands, must allow the appearance of the weight of the arrangement to be near the floor.

FOCAL AREA. A centre of interest.

FOLIAGE. Leaves of plant, shrub or tree, with or without a stem.

FORM. A design element.

FORMAL ARRANGEMENT. A symmetrical arrangement, free-standing or frontal.

FOUND OBJECTS. Bric-a-brac, miscellaneous articles of decorative interest.

FRAME. An actual frame or a frame of reference enclosing a design or designated space.

FREE EXPRESSION. An artistic arrangement with a modern concept yet not fitting into any specified category.

FREE FORM. A freestyle arrangement of flowing lines, free-standing or frontal. There should be no angular or straight lines in the composition and no stoppage points which would arrest eye movement.

FREE-STANDING. An arrangement

which can be judged from every angle.

FREE STYLE. The material dictates the design which may have more than one area of interest. The design may or may not be free form; is radial and does not conform to traditional construction or geometric form.

FRUIT. In an artistic class this usually means fresh, not dried fruit and includes both edible and non-edible fruit, berries, nuts, tomatoes, eggplant, squash and gourds.

FUNERAL SHEAVES. See Wired work.

GRADATION. A sequence in which there is orderly, regulated change in size, form, space, colour, weight and texture. Successful designs achieve an easy gradation from solidity at the faced area to thinness at the extremities.

HARMONY. A unity where all the elements of the composition fit together without jarring. A consistent, orderly, pleasing arrangement of parts.

HORSESHOE. A design shaped like a horseshoe, widening at the central focal area and narrowing to a point at each end.

HORTICULTURAL MATERIAL. Plant material, either living or dead; for example, weathered wood, twigs, dried or preserved leaves, fruit, berries, seed-pods, pussywillow bulrushes, etc.

HUE. A pure colour without the addition of either black or white.

INCORPORATING. Including but not featuring.

INFORMAL ARRANGEMENT. An arrangement in which balance is created by the asymmetrical placement of material.

INTEREST EQUATED. Interest is equated throughout the arrangement. There is more than one point of emergence, either from the container or the arrangement.

INTERMEDIATE HUES. Hues between the primary and secondary ones and which bear the name of both, for example, yellow-green or red-violet.

INTERPRETATIVE DESIGN. A design in which the elements are constructed so as to suggest a given theme.

LINE ARRANGEMENT. A design that features line.

MINIATURE ARRANGEMENT. A small arrangement in which flowers, foliage, container, base and accessories are in perfect proportion. The schedule usually states the minimum and maximum sizes allowed which are usually from 7 cm to 12 cm.

MIXED. If a schedule specifies ''mixed'', which it often does in formal work directions, at least three different kinds of flowers must be used.

MOBILE. A hanging construction or sculpture of delicately balanced moveable parts. The mobile should appear to float in the air rather than just to hang. The aim should be to achieve some beauty of movement.

MODERN. Bold, tailored, with dramatic impact.

MODERN MASS. A mass of material organised into a design of modern concept which may be symmetrical or

Opposite: A modern mass arrangement using tall pieces of wood with pink carnations massed at the base with aralia leaves.

asymmetrical. It must have great depth; planned space is a vital part of the design, emphasising mass. Materials are grouped according to type, colour, etc., without use of transition in the traditional manner. Flowers are placed at unusual angles and outline material is contrived into interesting silhouettes.

MONOCHROMATIC. Tints, shades and tones of one hue only.

MULTIPLE EMERGENCE. The components emerge from more than one point in the container or arrangement.

MULTIPLE HEAD. A cluster of flowers and/or bracts emerging from one stem.

NEUTRAL COLOURS. Black, white and grey.

NICHE. A space which has a backing and which forms a recess. An arrangement set in a niche should occupy approximately two-thirds of the space and should not touch the sides or the back of the recess and should not protrude too far forward.

NOVELTY CONTAINER. An interesting container, not a vase or bowl. The material used should not subordinate the interest of the container.

ORIGINALITY (CREATIVITY). The newness of concept with regard to the design of the arrangement, the materials used and the manner in which they are combined.

OUTLINE. The silhouette or framework of an arrangement.

PAINTED MATERIAL. Painted or artificially coloured material which should be used strictly according to the schedule requirements.

PATTERN. The interior design of an arrangement and the silhouette of the arrangement against its background.

PEDESTAL ARRANGEMENT. This differs from ''an arrangement on a pedestal'' in that the pedestal is an integral part of the arrangement.

PERIOD. A designated historical era.

PLATES. The schedule usually says ''Design to represent a painted design or plate'' or ''Crescent on a plate or platter''. Flower heads, etc., are arranged, with or without water, leaving part of the plate showing.

POSIES. See Wired work.

PRESENTATION SHEAVES. See Wired work.

PRIMARY COLOURS. Red, yellow and blue.

PRINCIPLES OF DESIGN. The inherent and applied relationship of design elements.

PROPORTION. A design priciple. The relationship in size between the components of a composition.

RADIAL. The central point of emergence from the focal area of the container.

REPETITION. The repeated use of size, form, colour, direction, etc.

RHYTHM. An illusion of movement through the arrangement created by the use of repetition, gradation and line direction.

SAUCER. A ''floral saucer'' is a slightly domed arrangement of flowers and leaves set in wet sand or something similar on a saucer. The border of leaves and/or petals should just cover the edge of the saucer. Colour-blending, scale and finish are very important. A ''decorated saucer'' is the same as above but accessories may be incorporated.

SCULPTURAL. Clean-cut forms presenting a chiselled or modelled effect.

SEAWEED. Marine plant-life.

SHADE. The "dark" value of a hue; a mixture of pure hue and black. The opposite of "tint".

SILHOUETTE. The outline pattern of an arrangement against its background.

SIMPLICITY. Nothing essential is omitted from the design and nothing is added which would detract from it.

SOLIDS. Anything with length, breadth and density.

SPACE. The open areas in and immediately around the arrangement. The three-dimensional expanse within which an arrangement is organised.

SPONGES. Marine animal life. They can be used as accessories.

SPRAYS. See Wired work.

STABILE. An arrangement which has stability and, although motionless, looks as though it might suddenly move — "arrested motion". It may be free-standing or frontal.

STAMOBILE. An arrangement in which a mobile and stabile are included in the same composition. The mobile may be attached to the stabile or hang from above to form an integral part of the design.

STILL LIFE. Although a traditional concept in the art of painting, this is a modern concept in floral art. It is an arrangement of plant material and objects of everyday life to present a unified, aesthetic grouping. Like the assemblage with which it has some affinity, it may be non-objective or expressive. The theme is interpreted more by the objects used than the plant material, although the plant material may predominate. Figurines are not generally used, the objects being actual in size and true to their function.

SYMMETRICAL ARRANGEMENT. An arrangement with the balance of interest equally distributed on either side of a central imaginary axis.

TALL ARRANGEMENT.
An arrangement of tall, slender material in an upright or shallow container and which emphasises the ascending movement of the design. It can exceed the usual height.

TECHNIQUE. Method of construction.

TEXTURE. The quality of surface construction, for example, rough, smooth, dull, shiny. It should be considered with regard to plant material, containers and accessories.

THEME. The subject of a composition.

TINT. The "light" value of a hue; a mixture of pure hue and white. The opposite of "shade".

TONE. A hue that has been changed by the addition of grey.

TRADITIONAL ARRANGEMENT. An arrangement constructed according to the fashion of the past. Twentieth-century traditional arrangements may be symmetrical or asymmetrical and may take the shape of arcs, curves, fans, ovals, stars, quadrilaterals, etc.

TRANSITION. The gradual stepping up or down of size, form, colour or texture.

TRIANGLE. A symmetrical floral triangle has equal balance of visual weight on each side of an imaginary axis. An asymmetrical

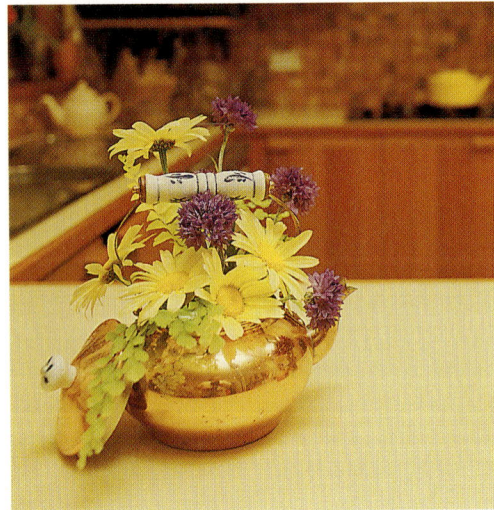

Top: An antique ruby glass container containing sprays of phaelenopsis with one green aralia leaf. The rose-quartz figures and amethyst tree pick up the colours of the arrangement. Above: Blue delphiniums, pink roses, carnations and white candytuft arranged in a yachting trophy. An arrangement of this type looks lovely in a lounge room.

Top: The swirling lines on the container are accentuated by the curved branches of the pussywillow and the downward curve of the pink-ruffled gladiolus. The royal-blue and pink theme is echoed by the dishes on the dresser.
Above: The blue on the handles of a copper kettle is picked up by cornflowers, while the yellow daisies tone with the colour scheme of the kitchen.

A contrast in colour and texture. The soft orange and yellow blooms of lilliums contrast with the blue walls and the rough texture of the rock which hides the cupholder while blending with the slate base. Swirls of pussywillow provide movement.

triangle has off-centre balance.

UNITY. A harmonious blending of all the components of a design.

URN. A footed container of classical proportions which may or may not have handles. Shapes range from squat to tall and slender.

VALUE. The intensity of a colour.

VARIATION. The change in the use of space, form, texture, colour, size and length of stem to avoid monotony in an arrangement. Licence may be taken with "modern arrangements".

VASE. A container with greater height than width.

VERTICAL ARRANGEMENT. An arrangement with an upright direction and rhythm of the internal pattern. If arranged in a shallow container the arrangement may come to, but not extend beyond, the side rims. If an arrangement is in an upright container the widest part may extend to about one-quarter the width of the container on either side.

VICTORIAN POSY. See Wired work.

VOIDS. The spaces between the solid elements of a design. They should vary in shape and size to form a pattern and should never look haphazard.

WIRED WORK. Arrangements which are not required to last for more than a few days and which are held together by invisible wire. See the "Wired work" section below.

WREATHS. See Wired work.

WIRED WORK

Wired work requires considerable technique as, unlike most other arrangements, it has to be handled, often for a length of time. All these made-up pieces should look as natural as possible with no unsightly wires in evidence. It is particularly important to use flowers and foliage that are at their best; poor material collapses quickly and no matter how good the design, points will be lost if a judge cannot pick up and examine an exhibit without it beginning to fall apart. Finish is extremely important. Care must be taken with every detail; design, proportion, weight, colour and harmony.

BOUQUETS

A bunch of flowers that is round or nearly round, with or without trails as specified in the schedule. The centre should be raised, and the finish should be neat with wires covered or hidden. The bouquet should balance well when held in the hand.

BRIDAL SHEAVES

The sheaf of flowers must be dainty and fresh with only clean stems showing. All thorns must be removed. The design should have a raised focal area with no gap in the centre. Originality will gain points.

FUNERAL SHEAVES

Materials may be pegged to an oblong base. Design can be symmetrical with an equal distribution of material each side of a raised focal area of particularly beautiful flowers. A ribbon bow is permissible. An alternative is a natural-looking sheaf of flowers with a raised focal area, asymmetrical in design and firmly tied with twine.

POSIES

There are types to suit all occasions. A posy is an arrangement of small flowers and is approximately 23 cm in diameter over all. The schedule should state its requirements in this respect. Wired stems are not covered unless arranged in the looser type of design. A posy may be finished with a frill of tulle, lace, paper doily or ring of leaves or ribbon loops.

A "Victorian posy" is a slightly domed concentric circle of small flowers not less than 12 cm and not more than 15.5 cm in diameter. The outer edge should be finished with leaves only. The back may be neatened with a paper cone. The handle must be covered with ribbon and a small replica of the posy may be attached to the end of it together with some ribbon streamers. The handle should be bent.

PRESENTATION BASKETS

The flowers in the basket should be wired, firmly pegged and arranged to face the front unless the schedule says the basket is to be viewed from all angles. The backing, usually of leaves, should be flat. Only good-quality material, well-conditioned, should be used. The basket should be light enough to be carried and two-thirds of the handle should be free to allow easy handling. The handle may be free to allow easy handling. The handle may be finished with a ribbon bow or a small flower spray.

PRESENTATION SHEAVES

The design should have a raised focal area. The stems may or may not be enclosed in a cellophane wrapping. Ribbon ties should be clean and crisp.

SPRAYS

The back of the spray arrangement must be flat so that it does not roll to the side when lying on the bench. Wires should not be visible.

WREATHS

Only long-lasting material should be used. The flowers, etc., must be firmly wired and pegged to a base of oasis or a moss-covered wire frame with a round opening in the centre. Wire and pegging should be invisible. The design should be slightly domed. Judgement is made on design, colour, freshness, technique and finish.

CHAPTER NINE

FLOWER TALK

I n Victorian times when a lover sent flowers to a lady he often conveyed a secret message. Here is a list of the flowers and the sentiment they represent.

Acacia, yellow
Secret love

Almond, flowering
Hope

Anemone
Forsaken

Apple blossom
Preference

Azalea
Temperance

Bachelors button
Single blessedness

Balsam
Impatience

Balsam, red
Touch me not

Bay leaf
I change but in death

Bay leaf wreath
Reward of merit

Begonia
Dark thoughts

Belladonna
Silence

Bluebell
Constancy

Broom
Neatness, humility

Buttercup
Childishness, ingratitude

Calceolaria
Keep this for my sake

Campanula
Gratitude

Candytuft
Indifference

Canterbury bell
Acknowledgement

Carnation, red
Alas, my poor heart

Carnation, striped
Refusal

Carnation, yellow
Disdain

Cardinal flower
Distinction

China aster, single
I will think of it

China rose
Beauty always new

Chrysanthemum, red
I love

Chrysanthemum, yellow
Slighted love
Chrysanthemum, white
Truth
Cineraria
Ever bright
Clover, four-leafed
Be mine
Clover, white
Think of me
Columbine
Folly
Columbine, purple
Resolution
Coreopsis
Always cheerful
Crocus, spring
Youth, gladness
Crocus, saffron
Mirth
Cyclamen
Diffidence
Daffodil
Regard
Daffodil, great yellow
Chivalry
Dahlia, single
Good taste
Daisy, double
Participation
Daisy, white
Innocence
Dandelion
Oracle
Daphne
Painting the lily
Dogwood
Durability

Fern
Sincerity

Forget-me-not
True love

Foxglove
Insincerity

French marigold
Jealousy ·

Fuschia, scarlet
Taste

Garland of roses
Reward of virtue

Geranium, ivy
Bridal favour

Geranium, rose or pink
Preference

Gladiolus
Strength of character

Heart's-ease
You occupy my thoughts

Heath
Solitude

Hibiscus
Delicate beauty

Honesty
Honesty

Honeysuckle
Bonds of love

Hyacinth, white
Unobtrusiveness, loveliness

Hydrangea
Boaster

Ice plant
Your looks freeze me

Iris
Message

Jasmine, white
Amiability

Jasmine, yellow
Grace and elegance

Jonquil
I desire a return of affection

Larkspur
Fickleness

Laurel
Glory

Lemon
Zest

Lilac, purple
First emotion of love

Lilac, white
Youthful innocence

Lily, yellow
Gaiety

Lily-of-the-valley
Return of happiness

Lucerne
Life

Marigold
Grief

Michaelmas daisy
Afterthought

Mignonette
Your qualities surpass your charms

Mistletoe
I surmount difficulties

Morning glory
Affection

Narcissus
Egotism

Narcissus, double
Female ambition

Nasturtium
Patriotism

Nemophila
I forgive you

Orange blossom
Your purity equals your loveliness

Palm
Victory

Pansy
Thoughts

Parsley
Festivity

Pelargonium, white
Gracefulness

Pelargonium, red
Her smile the soul of witchery

Peony
Shame, bashfulness

Petunia
Never despair

Phlox
Unanimity

Pinks
Boldness

Pink, single
Pure love

Pink, variegated
Refusal

Pink, white
Ingenious talent

Polyanthus
Pride of riches

Poppy, oriental
Silence

Poppy, red
Consolation

Primrose
Diffidence

Quince
Temptation

Ranunculus
You are radiant with charms

Rose
Love

Rose, cabbage
Ambassador of love

Rose, deep red
Bashfulness, shame

Rose, single
Simplicity

Rose, yellow
Decrease of love, jealousy

Roses, white and red together
Unity

Rosebud, deep red
Pure and lovely

Rosebud, white
A heart ignorant of love

Rosemary
Rememberance

Saffron
Mirth

Salvia, red
Forever thine

Salvia, blue
I think of you

Saxifrage
Affection

Scilla, blue
Forgive and forget

Snowdrop
Hope

Stephanotis
You can boast too much

Stock
Lasting beauty

Sunflower, tall
Haughtiness

Sunflower, dwarf
Adoration

Sweet pea
Delicate pleasures and departure
Sweet william
Gallantry
Tansy, wild
I declare war against you
Thistle (Scotch)
Retaliation
Thrift
Sympathy
Tuberosa
Dangerous pleasures
Tulip, red
Declaration of love
Tulip, variegated
Beautiful eyes
Tulip, yellow
Hopeless love
Verbena, white
Pure and guileless
Violet, blue
Faithfulness
Wallflower
Fidelity in adversity
Waterlily
Purity of heart
Weigelia
Accept a faithful heart
White lily
Purity and modesty
Wisteria
I cling to thee
Xeranthemum
Cheerfulness under adversity
Zinnia
Thoughts of absent friends.

CHAPTER TEN

Modern Trends and Foliage

Modern floral art is more than arranging a few flowers to add colour and beauty to your home. Dramatic designs are created by using a variety of plants, fewer flowers and modern accessories.

Modern designs are not bound by rigid rules, but care is taken so that each bloom is exhibited in a way that allows full appreciation of its individual beauty. There is an avoidance of fuss. The lines of the design are clean and uncluttered. Foliage can be used to lend shape and clarity to the 'modern' or abastract design. The soft beauty of one or two flowers combined with foliage carefully shaped for effect can be used to make arrangements which are delightfully 'different'.

Palms have stiff strong fronds which are easy to trim into different shapes. The line drawings show them cut into rounded shapes, fans and arrows. Two fern 'fans' can be joined to form a circle.

You can make your own shapes; taper the fronds; leave some tall ones in the centre and trim each side tightly. Be inventive.

Above: Curved pussy willow with a single camellia bloom. Right: Elkhorn, agapanthus and sygnonium on a redwood base.

The spathes of the palms can be used too. The tips can be left pointed or cut straight across. The stems are also useful.

CAMELLIA FOLIAGE

Camellias are used in modern designs. The stems should be stripped of all unnecessary leaves to that the base stems can be bent into a decorative shape.

Paper clips can be used to position a leaf where it is needed and can be hidden behind the flower.

Camellias are delicate flowers. You may need to use hair-spray lacquer to prevent the petals falling or even use a steel pin to hold the flower together.

FERNS

Ferns can be used to give a modern touch by stripping the fronds from one side. They can then be bent into shape and held in position with fine wire or nylon fishing line.

Many different effects can be achieved quickly and easily.

Fine florist's wire can be twisted through the design to help hold ferns in a desired position.

Foliage ''flowers'' can be made by clustering single leaves together and taping them on to a stem or stick. The ''flower'' can be used as the focal point of a foliage arrangement.

This ploy is useful when flowers are scarce, and autumn leaves offer a wide variety of colour as an attractive substitute.

FLAX

Flax, the long stiff pointed foliage is easy to split, trim and manipulate. I used it to great effect to follow the design of a lovely light-fitting. I split the leaves into long thin strips, tied the bundle together at top and bottom then spread the strips out into a balloon shape and painted them gold. Flax can be sprayed with paint — chrome, gold, silver, any colour you please. The strips can be looped to make 'ribbon bows'. It is easy to pierce, so you can thread it back through itself and create different shapes.

PUSSY WILLOW

Pussy willow is best used before the buds get too large and while the stems are supple. A steady pressure of the thumbs and forefingers of both hands will gently curve the pliant stem into a graceful curve. Use several stems together as shown in the drawings and combine the shapes. Both low and tall arrangements can be given movement and life in the simplest way. You will find that just one single bloom is all that is needed to turn a pussy willow curve into a graceful design.

The stems dry hard and will last for a full season. They can be used in their natural state or sprayed with colour.

Lovely bridal arrangements can be made using pussy willow sprayed with silver chrome paint with pure white flowers and trails of silvered ivy.

You can wire the stems into the shapes and circles you wish while they are growing on the tree so that when you need them, you have exact shapes ready for cutting. Rolling live stems or pliant branches around a bottle will give you attractive swirls to be used as decoration.

Pussy willow (before the buds get too large) bends easily and can be used to give curve and rhythm to an arrangement. Using a steady pressure of the thumb and first finger of both hands to make the curves or circles.

ABSTRACT ARRANGEMENTS

Monsterio foliage is ideal. Split the leaf in half for use in an abstract design.

Most modern arrangements radiate from one point — abstract arrangements can have two or more points of emergence.

Abstract arrangements depend on shape with foliage stripped to the minimum. Rounded flower-heads in brilliant colours make bold statements.

Strong-stemmed dahlias, stripped of leaves with only the shape and colour of the flowers creating the design can look stunning.

It is best to combine strong colour in an abstract arrangement; i.e. bright yellow, reds and orange with black and white.

MOBILES

Dried flowers, leaves and seed pods or fresh flowering heads in Oasis can be suspended from the ceiling by nylon fishing line with swivels holding the small arrangements in place, but allowing the slightest movement of air to move them slowly and gracefully.

Flower arrangements placed near a mobile are enhanced by the gentle movement.

STABILES

Skilful placement of materials in an arrangement set high on a stand or rod can create an illusion of movement. The arrangement must be able to be viewed from all sides. The 'floating' effect is enhanced if the tall rod is painted black or silver or made of clear perspex.

COLLAGES

A wall plaque made using dried flowers, leaves and seed pods can be very effective. The design can be abstract, the background bright. If you link the collage with an arranagement using fresh flowers and leaves of the same varieties, it gets a feeling of unity. This idea can be expanded to create a whole wall of design several metres high.

Top: Flax foliage is cut into strips to form a circle and sprayed with gold paint.

Above: From left to right : monstera leaf; blackboy foliage; A shaped palm-frond; dried clipped palm.

Top: Any variety of palm frond can be used clipped, shaped or dried and painted.

Above: Agapanthus flowers and stalks dry well and can be used in a variety of shapes.

An arrangement of red anthuriums is balanced by the height of the white peacock feathers in this tall perspex container.

The contrast in colour and shape of the blackened agapanthus triangles highlights the strelitzias in this arrangement.

INDEX